The Neteru of Kemet

An Introduction
2010 Electronic Edition

Tamara L. Siuda

The 2010 edition of The Neteru of Kemet: An Introduction was published by Stargazer Design and Lulu Press. Its text, excepting the addition of a foreword and minor changes to the layout to fit a new format, is otherwise identical to the first edition published in 1994 by Eschaton.

For information about permission to reproduce selections from this book, or to inquire about review copies, write to the author in care of Stargazer Design, 2328 E. Lincoln Highway, Suite 108, New Lenox, IL 60451.

Library of Congress Cataloging-in-Publication Data is available.
ISBN 978-0-557-34323-2
Softcover and Ebook edition

Printed in the United States of America

ISBN 978-0-557-34323-2
90000

9 780557 343232

FOREWORD TO THE 2010 EDITION

The Neteru of Kemet was initially written in 1993 and published in 1994 as a workbook for a class I was teaching on ancient Egyptian religion at a local New Age bookstore. It was written for that audience, and reflects not only the things they were interested in, but my own knowledge of the gods and their religion 17 years ago, before I went to graduate school and finished two master's degrees and got started on my doctorate in Egyptology. In my current state of research, this book feels rather like the essay one unearths from childhood days and wonders who the writer was, until she notes her own handwriting on the pages.

Why reprint something that is not only academically immature, but maybe even a little embarrassing to me? There are several reasons. One is that the "rare book market" that came up when the publisher went bankrupt and auctioned off the few remainders has gotten completely out of control for a book of this scope or length. The second, and perhaps more important reason, is that it represents a piece of curiosity and history for the Kemetic Orthodox Faith which I founded in 1989 and which was legally recognized as a religion in the USA the same year *Neteru* was released.

The House of Bast became the House of Netjer before the book even hit the shelves, and the rest of our history is written elsewhere, but for those of my students curious about what things were like when we started out, *Neteru* might be an interesting conversation piece, if nothing else. I am told that it is also an important document for the history of the "reconstructionist" movement that encompassed the revival of many ancient faiths including that of Kemet, even if I know I could write it better today.

Enjoy, but please do so knowing that I have reproduced *everything* here from the original design files, including my own amateur line art and all typos and factual errors. Nothing has been changed from the 1994 publication except the loss of that really nice-looking gold foil cover, and clip art replacements of some files that were irretrievably corrupted in transition from Pagemaker to InDesign. I opted to recreate over making a PDF of a scanned copy of the original as the scans got too big.

Rev. Tamara L. Siuda
Nisut of the Kemetic Orthodox Faith
The House of Netjer, PO Box 11188, Chicago, IL 60611-0188 USA

The Neteru of Kemet

An Introduction

Tamara Siuda-Legan

TABLE OF CONTENTS

INTRODUCTION

Three thousand years before the birth of Jesus Christ and perhaps even before, a civilization thrived on the banks of the Nile River in northern Africa that was called by its inhabitants *Kemet* ("Black Land"). This land is known today by the Greek name *Egypt*. By virtue of extensive archaeological study, we know a great deal about this ancient culture which in some ways was more advanced than our own; a culture that embraced multiple expressions of Deity, provided for social equality across race and gender, boasted of a government and civil service to rival that of ancient China; and had a remarkably practical religious philosophy.

THE BLACK LAND

"The water stands and fails not, and the Nile carries a high flood. The days are long, the nights have hours, and the months come aright. The Gods are content and happy of heart, and life is spent in laughter and wonder."

Sallier Papyrus, Erman translation

The religious system that existed in differing forms throughout Kemet's history spanned several thousand years, undergoing many changes. At one point, it can even be said to have been monotheist in nature. However, for the majority of Kemet's people, it was understood that there were many gods and goddesses—the *(Nedjeru* or *Neteru)* of one's city, profession and clan as well as greater *Neteru* whose celebrations were marked by the entire populace. *Neteru* (singular *Neter)* is a Kemetic word that translates "powers" or "divinities," much in the same sense of a term used by another indigenous African religion: the *Orishas* of the Yoruba nations. *Neteru* is a word without gender and can stand for either God or Goddess, as well as Gods or Goddesses. The people of Kemet saw the creative influence of *Neteru* in all things, including themselves.

Though there were more than 200 different rulers (both male and female), at least three major foreign occupations and many rewritings of "official" history, philosophy and religious dogma, the faith of both the people and the priest(ess)hood of Kemet was highly celebratory and life-affirming. Though different *Neteru* were worshipped under different rulers and from place to place, They all had something in common: They were accessible to all and to each other, and Their worship covered every facet of life, from conception to death to rebirth and everything in between.

When one looks at archaeological finds and notes from early Egyptologists, it appears that the religion of Kemet was little more than a death cult with the process of mummification at its apex. This is not so. Because subsequent civilizations destroyed or co-opted most of Kemet's temples and shrines, often the tombs are our most reliable surviving evidence of Kemet's religious practices. For example, a text central to Kemetic religion, known today as the *Book of the Dead,* as copies of it were found in almost every tomb after the Second Intermediate Period, is not a "book" at all. It is a collection of writings more accurately titled *Chapters of Going Forth by Day* and details life and spiritual transformation, both in this world and the next.

For the people of Kemet, life was a joyous celebration of *Ma'at,* the Goddess and the concept of Truth, Justice and Order. *Neteru* were as accessible as the nearest temple, village chapel or household shrine—or in the life-giving rays of the sun, the "hands" of the Aten or Ra; the song of a scarab beetle, symbol of Khepera, the Self-Created One; the meow of a kitten, sacred to Lady Bast; or in the lumbering gait of a crocodile, the animal dedicated to Sebek, Lord of the Nile. *Neteru* were in everything and *were everything*—one was never alone. The concept of "Two Lands" or "Twin Lands"—more than just geographic designations of Lower and Upper Kemet— spoke of an interconnectedness between the "land" of one's material and spiritual lives—the "lands" of earth and the "land" of the *Neteru.*[1] For the people of Kemet there was no separation of sacred and secular life—everything was an expression of the sacred and was revered as *Neter.* Any member of society could interact with *Neteru,* from a household servant to the Pharaoh, the Living embodiment of the Great God Heru; or the Great Queen, His consort, the Living Goddess. The priest(ess)hood existed to serve the people of Kemet and bring them in touch with *Neteru* by virtue of their extensive training (which sometimes took decades), to enact sacred dramas and maintain the sacred texts, and to serve the Great House of Pharaoh and His Queen by acting as royal stand-ins in all temples across the Two Lands.

Although it influenced neighboring cultures (Greeks, Hebrews and Romans among them), the religion of Kemet was assimilated by later faiths and finally disappeared as sand buried the temples and later civilizations and religions forbade the worship of the *Neteru.* As people forgot how to read the hieroglyphic texts, other knowledge of this long and prosperous civilization was lost as well. And at the burning of the Alexandrian Libraries, the last repository of ancient Near Eastern learnings, in the Sixth Century CE, it seemed the religion of Kemet would be lost forever.

THE RELIGION OF KEMET TODAY

"As long as the heavens last, so shall you last."

—spoken by the Great God Anpu to Pharaoh Seti I,
in his chapel to the Goddess Aset,
19th Dynasty, New Kingdom (ca 1300 BCE)

Between the 16th and 18th Centuries CE, Westerners, including Napoleon, set foot on Egyptian soil and took in the wonders of monuments time could not erase: the Sphinx and Pyramids at Giza, more pyramids at Dashur and Memphis, and the ruined temples, tombs and buildings at Philae, Dendera, Karnak and many other sites. Scholars from several Western nations set to work deciphering the strange pictorial notations on these monuments, and slowly (more quickly after Cham-pol-lion's breakthrough with the Rosetta Stone), the culture, history and religion of the land of Kemet emerged. Religious texts were translated and revealed to the world once more, in all their glory, a living system that had survived the ravages of time: a religious philosophy that honored life and all things subsequent world religions have held as "good"—a system and a Pantheon *which are still valid* for those called to them.

Through study with persons in the fields of Egyptology, anthropology, history and the direct request of the *Neteru* Themselves, the priest(ess)hood of Kemet is return-ing to the world. They are dedicated to the service of the *Neteru,* Who after all this time still answer most heartily to human voices! Even if the religion of Kemet is not for you, an understanding of its basic tenets and thoughts (which bear resemblance to the philosophy of a contemporary ancient system: the *Tao* of the ancient Chinese) offers insight into what it is to be human and what celebrations life has to offer, ideas central to all faith structures.

The Neteru of Kemet: An Introduction is exactly that. This workbook is intended as an adjunct to personal study and meditation on the *Neteru,* not as a total overview of the Kemetic religion. It is best used by a person who is either already familiar with the history and philosophy of Kemet or who is interested in learning of the *Neteru* and Their expression. While it would be impossible to discuss all of the *Neteru* (there are several thousand), the 13 Goddesses and Gods described in the following pages are some of the most universally-known *Neteru* and those Whose followings extend-ed throughout much if not all of the Two Lands, and in some cases beyond (for example, ruins of a Roman temple to *Aset* [*Isis* in Greek] have been uncovered in London). Meditative work with these *Neteru* can provide a sound introduction to the religion of Kemet, as all of Them are readily accessible to the sincere seeker. (An important note: "sincere" in the Kemetic philosophy does *not* mean addressing *Neter* as an archetype or focus point of the Higher Self, known as the *ka* or "double." As in other indigenous African religions, *Neteru* are actual spiritual beings and do not respond favorably to New Age philosophy's "I am God/dess" arrogance.)

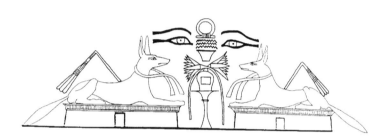

FOOTNOTES

[1]The "Twin Lands" principle/metaphor was elaborated on by Mistress Cara-Marguerite-Drusilla, L.P.H., of the House of Life KMT at the 1993 Parliament of World's Religions in her plenary presentation "Living in the Twin Lands." An article with my further commentary on the concept can be obtained from the House of Netjer, Post Office Box 11188, Chicago, IL 60611-0188 USA.

ACKNOWLEDGMENTS

I am grateful to: Rev. Phoebe Wray, Handmaiden of Sekhmet and Mistress Cara-Marguerite-Drusilla, L.P.H., Priestess Hierophant of the House of Life KMT in Ayer, Massachusetts, for all of their lessons and support; and am deeply indebted to Rev. Craig A. Schaefer, Servant of Bast, the Administrative Director of Ordo Alba Phoenix and my partner in the House of Bast, without whom this book would never have seen print.

I am also thankful for the written works and translations of Cyril Aldred, T. G. Allen, John Baines, James Henry Breasted, Normandi Ellis, R. O. Faulkner, John Foster, Alan Gardiner, Erik Hornung, Miriam Lichtheim, Edouard Naville, R. B. Parkinson, Michael Poe, Donald Redford, William Kelly Simpson and others. Unattributed references in this work are synthesized from what I learned both directly and indirectly from these women and men as well as what I learned from the *Neteru* Themselves, who brought me home.

May these words feed the *kas* of the *Neteru* and may my voice be true.

In Ma'at,

Rev. Tamara Siuda-Legan, Handmaiden of Bast
The House of Bast
Member Temple, Ordo Alba Phoenix

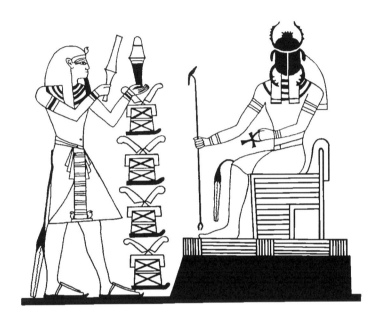

THE KEMETIC "RELIGION"

"Religion," when used in relation to the faith practices and philosophies of Kemet, is actually a misleading term. Throughout a culture that extended more than 3,000 years, religion both from the standpoint of the state and of the common people underwent more than a few major changes. However, there were some constants throughout Kemetic history that bear notice, as well as a look at the differentiation between the popular creeds and a look at the difference between faith practice for a noble or a ruler and that of the general citizenry, and finally, a look at the Kemetic faith through the eyes of some of today's practitioners.

Most of what is known to us about the religious practice of Kemet in antiquity has been preserved in the funerary and liturgical texts pertaining to the state religion—the religion of Pharaoh. As the embodiment of the Great *Neter* Heru (or in later times, Amen-Ra), the Pharaoh along with his Great Queen (a living reflection of the *Neter* Tefnut, Het-hert or Aset, depending on time and dynastic emphasis) were considered the primary conduits to the *Neteru*. In every temple in Kemet the royal pair were expected to perform the daily religious rituals on behalf of their people and their land. Of course, as it was not possible for them to make an appearance twice daily in every single temple, trained priests and priestesses served as proxy in their stead.

The state-designated temples of Kemet were awesome structures, some of them existing, albeit in ruined form, even today. At the beginning of Kemet's history temples were simple wooden shrines containing an image or symbol of a *Neter*, progressing to small stone shrines with a tall flag and the symbol of the *Neter* on a pole (hence the hieroglyph for *Neter*, ᨤ which resembles a flag). Eventually these shrines were surrounded by low walls, and these walls by more walls, columns and gates ("pylons"), the legacies of Pharaoh after Pharaoh, until in the New Kingdom, some temple precincts extended more than a mile in length. The "typical" New Kingdom state temple consisted of an entirely walled complex, approached by a wide road flanked by sphinxes or other statues. Right inside the first pylon would be a wide open courtyard, where any member of society could come to witness public rites and sacred dramas and to participate in festivals. Beyond the courtyard, another pylon led to a *hypostyle* or columned hall with small windows near the roof. At the end of the hypostyle hall would be another pylon, leading to three (sometimes more) adjacent sanctuaries containing the sacred images, shrines and processional bark of the *Neter* (and His or Her "family") to which the temple was dedicated. For example, in a temple of Amen-Ra these three rooms were for Amen-Ra, His consort Mut and Their son Khonsu. Only a Pharaoh, Great Queen, or member of the trained priest(ess)hood, *Hem-Neter* or Servant of *Neter* (feminine *Hem(e)t-Neter* or Handmaiden of *Neter),* could enter the sanctuary; in fact, only members of the priest(ess)hood and the royal family could progress past the outer courtyard and into the temple. (In order that the common folk's prayers would still be heard, some temples were equipped with holes in the wall between the temple and courtyard with drawings of ears above them: a person could whisper his or her prayer into the hole and it would be carried into the sanctuary by a priest/ess standing inside listening for that purpose.) Around or behind the main temple but still within the containment walls would be buildings for storing temple goods and offerings, the library, the treasury and housing for the resident priest(ess)hood and their families, as well as gardens, groves and artificial lakes or pools.

Light played a major role in many temples, even for temples to *Neteru* without obvious affinities to light or darkness. Most temples grew progressively dimmer until one reached the sanctuary, which was completely dark—notable exceptions were the Temple to the Aten (Sun-Disk) in Akhetaten, which was roofless and completely laid open to sunlight; and the Great Temple of Bast in Per-Bast (*Bubastis* in Greek), consisting of a wall surrounding a large garden oasis and a grove of trees, in the center of which stood Bast's shrine.

A sanctuary was the sacred earthly dwelling of the *Neter* to which it was dedicated. Inside a shrine, a gilded wood or stone rectangular container often resting on a pillar or altar top, an image of the *Neter* was kept. In temples where sacred animals associated with a particular *Neter* were raised, these would also be allowed to enter the sanctuary. Also kept in the sanctuary was the processional bark: a miniature boat carried with poles by a battery of priests and/or priestesses, in which the *Neter* and Its shrine would be carried for festivals requiring It to leave the temple, either to visit another temple or for a parade about the city in which It was worshipped. The shrine was considered as holy as the image of the *Neter* itself—even though surviving representations of bark processions show that the shrine doors were generally not opened to reveal the image within, the people see the glory of the Neter in the procession, called an "appearance" or "going forth."[1]

There are many texts describing oracular messages received by both commoners and royalty from the sacred image of a *Neter* during these processions. In later Kemet these images were consulted on a regular basis on petitions and legal cases, where texts say they "gave their assent" or "denied permission" regarding questions put to them. Some archaeologists theorize that these statues were fitted with strings or levers, enabling them to nod or shake their heads. While few images of *Neteru* found to date support this theory, it is indeed possible, as is an explanation offered by the texts themselves: the priests bearing the image "felt" the correct answer and moved forward or backward according to what they were "told" by the *Neter*. Either way, sacred images were credited with a number of successful cases, including criminal investigations in which they singled out guilty parties and pardoned the innocent; and some New Kingdom Pharaohs claimed to have been validated or directed by Amen Himself through consultation of an oracle.[2]

The state religion was brought to the people of Kemet on a number of occasions, not the least of which were the processions of sacred images. There were also a number of public festivals and sacred dramas in which any interested person could take part. In fact, some city festivals were said to be so large that in them, "all the women who are in the city act as priestesses, and they have since the days of the fathers."[3]

In these sacred dramas which often took a number of days to complete, people from all over Kemet would come to a temple to re-enact a myth pertaining to Its *Neter*; for example, the drama of the death and resurrection of Ausar (Osiris) by Aset (Isis) was reenacted annually at several temples over at least a six-day period.

Any person could make an offering to a temple—of food, flowers, wine, water, perfume or other precious objects or materials—whatever (s)he saw fit. The gift would be presented to the *Neter* in Its shrine by the Servant or Handmaiden of the *Neter,* and then in the case of food or money, taken to the priest(ess)hood for their sustenance or to the treasury. Gifts of perfume, jewels or precious materials would be used for temple furniture or in the daily ritual in the temple on the *Neter's* behalf.

Kemetic daily rituals have the same structure regardless of the *Neter* they honor. In the morning, the Servant or Handmaiden of the *Neter* enters the sanctuary, either alone or, optimally, after a *Web* (purification priest/ess) has cleansed the area with water and incense, and greets the *Neter* by kneeling or laying on the floor before the shrine. Once invocations have been said and certain physical gestures made, the shrine is opened and the image brought forth, where It is reclothed, makeup and jewelry applied to Its body, and It is "fed" offerings from the priest(ess)hood and others. While the image of the *Neter* is attended to, Its shrine is purified with more incense and perfumes, and then it is returned to the shrine with more invocations and prayers. The same ritual minus the "feeding" is enacted again in the late evening. In some temples the Servant or Handmaiden goes to bed and awakens a few hours after midnight to do the evening liturgy.

In contrast to the formal structure of Kemet's state religion stands the religion of the common people. Unfortunately, because of its more private and less structured nature, there is little available historical information. It is generally accepted that most persons had a private altar or alcove in their homes dedicated to a *Neter* they deemed important, either the *Neter* of their family, profession or city. In some smaller towns where a member of a trained priest(ess)hood lived, "village shrines" were owned and operated by that particular priest/ess and other common folk who worshipped the same *Neter.* A village shrine was a one-room or open sanctuary with a private membership. Shrine membership was set up similarly to a modern fraternal organization or private club and included benefits such as sharing of debts and funeral expenses, festivals and potluck dinners. Shrine members carried out duties related to the essence or mission of the particular *Neter* the shrine was intended to honor; for example, a village shrine to Sekhmet might be dedicated to the practice of medicine, while a shrine to Aset would be dedicated to doing magic or midwifery. Village shrines were maintained by their members, sometimes with assistance from state temples or wealthy priests or priestesses of the same *Neter,* and did not "compete": a person could be a member of any shrine (s)he was interested in and village shrine membership did not preclude private or organized state worship.

Some *Neteru* were worshipped almost exclusively in private homes: *Bes,* the jovial dwarf god of happiness, protector of children and pregnant women; *Tauert,* hippopotamus goddess of childbirth who protected the bed and birthing-bricks of a woman in labor; and several other *Neteru* of protection and domestic bliss. A majority of homes also kept a shrine to their familial ancestors and visited the known tombs of ancestors in order to make offerings to the spirits of their blessed departed kin, who were considered to be as *Neteru* in the afterworld and demanding of the offerings and attention of the living.

Modern considerations and cultural changes have had to be made by current practitioners of Kemetic faith. These include a lack of a Nile-based agricultural society and the loss of many texts, open access to temples and the like. While differing Kemetic groups practice in different fashions, it may be useful to look at examples of one current group's practice to see the changes from and similarities to the traditional Kemetic religion.

The House of Bast works with a fairly solid reconstruction of Kemet's state (formal) religion as practiced before the Late Period (c. 1000 BCE), with the democratic and "free" elements of individual and village shrine worship mixed in. Temple members maintain their own shrines to whatever *Neter(u)* they serve and whenever possible, attend rituals at the main temple and shrine. The ordained priest(ess)hood of the House of Bast does not take special "privileges" over the general membership and any member can lead ritual as *kher-heb* ("lector-priest/ess" or the person who reads texts, makes invocations, etc.); serve the temple as *web* ("purification priest/ess," the person who purifies and prepares temple, tools and sacred space before ritual and closes the temple); or act as *sesh-per-ankh* (temple scribe). Training is rigorous and time-consuming (as in antiquity, the process of becoming a priest/ess takes years and sometimes decades); however, one's outside life is considered as important a lesson as one's temple/religious life, in the pragmatic spirit of the Two Lands. Liturgy is drawn from original sources and given in the Kemetic language whenever possible. If not feasible, an English translation is prepared with paraphrase if necessary to match the intuitive spirit of the liturgy being performed. Temple processions and sacred dramas are carried out, with all attendees taking part.

House of Bast temple dress is formal; robes and headdresses are common. Color, style and accessories/tools are left to the discretion of each member, according to historical research and the *Neter* (s)he serves; for example, a Handmaiden or Dedicant of Sekhmet might want to wear red robes, while a Servant or Dedicant of Ma'at would prefer white ones for purity. Most Kemetic robes and clothing historically were white, partly because of its association with Ma'at and purity, and partly for a pragmatic purpose: to stay cool in the desert sun. Some female members of the House of Bast carry sistra (ritual rattles) in temple or wear bells on their person to bring music and sound to temple, as was done in ancient times. Another ancient symbol and protective amulet, an ankh pendant, is worn as an outward sign of the Kemetic faith; and initiates wear scarabs, either as rings or pendants, for protection and in honor of the creative essence manifest in the *Neter* Khepera.

FOOTNOTES

[1]A description of the construction and the duties of the priesthood concerning sacred barks and processions is given in the Stele of Ikhernofret (Middle Kingdom), translated by Miriam Lichtheim in *Ancient Egyptian Literature* vol. 1, pp. 123-125.

[2]Eighteenth Dynasty Pharaohs Hatshepsut and Horemheb both claimed to be validated by Amen Himself (Hatshepsut declared herself His bodily daughter through a sacred marriage between Amen and her mother and Horemheb was said to be validated by the oracular statue of Amen at his coronation); and the entire Ramessid line (19th Dynasty) appended their Pharaohnic titles with *mery-Amen or sa-Amen* (beloved of Amen/son of Amen) instead of the ages-honored *sa Ra* (Son of Ra) as an outward sign of their affinity with the Great *Neter* of Thebes.

[3]*The Festival Hall of Osorkon II in the Great Temple of Bubastis*, Edouard Naville.
See "For Further Reading" for a full bibliography.

THE NETERU OF KEMET
VIGNETTES

The following are vignettes describing the epithets and mythologies surrounding 13 of the *Neteru* of Kemet. They are arranged in the same fashion: starting with some original texts on Their nature, followed by a short visualization/meditation to begin the approach to the essence of the *Neter* being described. Following this is a short discussion of the attributes, history and nature of the *Neter.*

Because of the mysterious, essentially "unknowable" nature of the Neteru and the multiple layers of meaning attached to each *Neter* according to the philosophy of Kemetic religion, it is to be understood that these vignettes *do not* represent a "total" view of the Neter they describe, or of the entire Kemetic religion. Instead they are intended as springboards for meditation and education, to begin your journey toward inner knowledge of the *Neteru* in your own life.

RA
(Amen-Ra, Khepera, Tem/Atum, Aten, Herukhuti)

"Hail to you, Herukhuti-Khepera, Who created Himself.
How beautiful is Your arising in the horizon,
illuminating the Two Lands with Your rays.
All Gods are in exultation when They see
the King of Heaven, the Lord,
with the Uraeus abiding on His forehead.
Its place is made as Your symbol of power,
and the crowns of Upper and Lower Kemet
are on Your brow."

—Stele for Tjeker-Tehuti, Ptolmaic-Roman Period
Field Museum of Natural History, Chicago

"Hail to Thee, Amen-Ra,
Who takes pleasure in truth."

—*Book of the Dead, or Going Forth by Day*
Utterance 15A (3b), T. G. Allen translation

"Arise, Ra. Arise Thou in Thy shrine,
so that Thou mayest engulf the winds,
inhale the north wind,
swallow the spine,
spit out the day,
kiss the truth."

—*The Book of the Two Ways*
Coffin Texts 1029, DeBuck translation

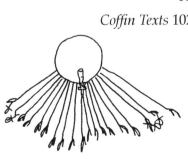

TAKE UP YOUR SEAT IN THE BOAT OF MILLIONS OF YEARS, LOOK OVER THE
SIDE AT THE WORLD GOING BY BELOW YOU, RELAX AND KNOW THAT THE BOAT
WILL RIDE SMOOTHLY AND YOU WILL ARRIVE AT THE HORIZON AT NIGHTFALL,
WHERE TEM WILL FOLD YOU GENTLY INTO HIS ARMS. TURN AROUND AND GAZE
ON THE FORM OF THE GREAT NETER RA, KINDLY, BRIGHT AND SHINING. AP-
PROACH RA. SPEAK WITH HIM IF YOU WILL. HE MAY APPEAR TO YOU AS THE
FALCON OF NOONTIDE, THE SCARAB KHEPERA OF SUNRISE, THE SELF-CREATED
TEM, THE ROUND YELLOW DISK OF THE ATEN, OR THE DIVINE KING, AMEN-RA
OF THE GOLDEN COUNTENANCE....

The Great *Neter* Ra, Father of Gods and Men, is one of the central *Neteru* of the Kemetic
Pantheon. At any given time in Kemet's history He was worshipped in a multiplicity of
forms and names, probably due to the pervasiveness of the natural symbol He claims
for His own: the bright golden orb of Earth's own sun. The celestial sun, as the Boat
of Millions of Years, carries Ra forward from His "birth" on the eastern horizon to His
"death" at sunset in the west. Ra's story does not end here—He is carried by His boat
through the dangers of the underworld while skies are dark, only to emerge blazing
from the eastern horizon the very next day in all His golden splendor.

Ra is a *Neter* of light and victory, of protection and of immeasur-
able power. As *Khepera* He is Creator, Who came forth from Himself; a light in the darkness, rolling life like a scarab rolls balls of
dung into the light, from which its children spring as if by magic.
As *Tem* or *Atum* He is the Creative Essence, the power of life and
time which carries forth desire into reality. As *Amen-Ra,* the Hidden Lord, He is both the bright and blazing light of truth and the
whispering wind of power. As *Herukhuti* (*Horakhthy* in Greek), He
soars through the sky as a falcon, seeing all, protecting the birds in
His nest.

Ra's power is infinite: by sheer force of will He created Himself as a *Bennu,* or phoenix, upon the mountain of creation. By knowledge of Ra's secret name, the Great *Neter* Aset becomes Mistress of Magic and equal to the most powerful Being in existence. Mating with Nut, the Vault of Stars and the Nighttime Sky, Ra fathers the five *Neteru* whose birthdays precede every new year: Ausar, Heru, Set, Aset and Nebet Het.

Ra is in the fire of sunshine, the cries of falcons, the willful, determined work of scarabs. Like the sun, He keeps us warm, offers life, marks the cycles of day and night, months and years, centuries and millennia. Yet as the sun can burn skin and plants, Ra can be violent and devastating. When mankind rebelled against Ra's rule, He sent out His Daughter Sekhmet that the evildoers might be punished—then took pity on them and called Her back. Rather than let the Great *Neter* Set be punished for the killing of His Brother Ausar, Ra gave Him a place at the prow of His Boat, where the *Neter* of Strength now fends off the serpent of chaos from the Lord of Limitless Light. Amen-Ra went into battle at the side of His son, Pharaoh Rameses II, protecting him from the armies of the Hittites at the Battle of Kadesh: "He gave me His hand, and I rejoiced," says Rameses' record of the battle on the walls of his temples to Amen.

TEHUTI
(DJEHUTI, THOTH)

"He is the Lord of Kindliness,
the leader of the entire multitude."

—from a schoolboy's notes, 18th Dynasty
British Museum collection 5656

"Give praise to Thoth;
make rejoicing to Him every day.
He Who gives breath to the weary-hearted one
and vindicates him against his enemies,
He vindicates you against your enemies."

—*Book of the Dead or Going Forth By Day*
Utterance 18, T. G. Allen translation

"The vizier Who settles cases,
Who changes turmoil to peace;
the scribe of the mat Who keeps the book,
Who punishes crime,
Who accepts the submissive,
Who is sound of arm,
wise among the Ennead;
Who relates what was forgotten."

—from a statue of Pharaoh Horemheb
18th Dynasty

ENTER THE LIBRARY OF TEHUTI, A LONG, DARK HALL FILLED FROM FLOOR TO CEILING WITH SHELVES FULL OF BOOKS IN ALL LANGUAGES, AND MANY ROLLED-UP SCROLLS. EVERYTHING THAT HAS EVER BEEN PUT IN INK TO PAPER IS IN THIS LIBRARY. AT THE FAR END, BELOW A WINDOW WHERE THE SUN SHINES IN, FILTERING THROUGH THE DUST OF A MILLION OLD TOMES, STANDS A MAN WITH AN IBIS HEAD. HE HAS HIS BACK TO YOU AND IS WRITING SOMETHING

ON A PIECE OF PAPYRUS WITH A PEN MADE FROM A SLENDER REED. AS YOU APPROACH, YOU CAN SEE WHAT HE IS WRITING, AND IF IT IS IN A LANGUAGE YOU DO NOT NORMALLY UNDERSTAND, SOMEHOW, THIS TIME, YOU CAN READ IT. TEHUTI TURNS AND LOOKS UPON YOU WITH THE BRIGHT, WISE EYES OF A BIRD—THE SAME EYES THAT HOLD THE KNOWLEDGE OF A MILLION YEARS....

In a society saturated with information in all its forms, it should not be difficult to relate to the Great *Neter* Tehuti. Tehuti presides over all forms of communication as Divine Scribe. He is credited with the creation of written language: *metu Neter,* the "words of God." He is Lord of Wisdom, one of the oldest *Neteru* of the Pantheon, in some of the mythologies even considered senior to Ra. Traditionally Tehuti is depicted with the head of an ibis, a bird found in great numbers along the banks of the Nile. An ibis has a singularly distinguished expression; its appearance of "seriousness" caused it to be associated with this Great *Neter.*

Tehuti has dominion over time: by playing a game of Senet with the moon, He was able to secure the five intercalary days during which the Divine Children of Ra and Nut could be born. He is also a divine judge, the consort of Ma'at, *Neter* and Concept of Truth, Justice and Order. Tehuti stands next to the scales upon which one's heart is weighed after death, prepared with his reed pen and papyrus scroll to record the result for eternity. A baboon, another of His symbols, sits at the scales as well, to be sure they are even.

Patron of scribes and judges, Tehuti offers knowledge of *ma'at* to all who will listen. He will protect those who are truthful, who carry *ma'at* in their hearts. He can answer any question—though sometimes in His infinite wisdom He may suggest that perhaps one does not want or need to know the answer. Tehuti's presence is overwhelming: He literally speaks volumes. No thing is hidden from the sharp eyes of this patient, wise *Neter*. Along with His other consort, Seshat, *Neter* of Records and Libraries, Tehuti records the names and deeds of all beings on the leaves of a sacred sycamore tree. What has He written on your leaf?

MA'AT
(MAYET)

"Ma'at is in every place that is yours....You rise with Ma'at, you live with Ma'at, you join your limbs to Ma'at, you make Ma'at rest on your head in order that She may take Her seat on your forehead. You become young again in the sight of your daughter Ma'at, you live from the perfume of Her dew. Ma'at is worn like an amulet at your throat; She rests on your chest, the Divine Entities reward you with Ma'at, for they know Her wisdom....

Your right eye is Ma'at, your left eye is Ma'at, your flesh, your members are Ma'at....Your food is Ma'at, your drink is Ma'at, the breaths of your nose are Ma'at....You exist because Ma'at exists and vice versa."

—Berlin Papyrus

BEFORE YOU ARE THE LARGEST PAIR OF SCALES YOU HAVE EVER SEEN. IN ONE PAN IS A LARGE WHITE OSTRICH FEATHER. AS YOU LOOK AT IT, A HAND REACHES FORTH TO PICK IT UP, AND YOU GAZE UPWARD TO FIND YOURSELF FACE TO FACE WITH MA'AT. SHE IS A WOMAN WITH LARGE MULTICOLORED WINGS, A GOLDEN ANKH IN ONE HAND AND A WHITE FEATHER, LIKE THE ONE FROM THE SCALE, BOUND TO HER HEAD WITH A GOLDEN CORD. SHE SAYS NOTHING, ONLY SMILES. YOU REALIZE THAT SHE IS WAITING FOR YOU TO SPEAK. POUR YOUR HEART OUT TO MA'AT. ANYTHING YOU NEED TO FEEL BETTER ABOUT, WRONGS THAT HAVE BEEN DONE TO YOU, WRONGS THAT YOU HAVE COMMITTED THAT YOU WANT TO MAKE AMENDS FOR—TELL HER. SHE HEARS IT ALL AND FORGIVES YOU. YOUR HEART IS ON THE OTHER PAN OF THE SCALE, AND WHEN SHE PLACES HER FEATHER BACK ON THE OTHER SIDE, THE PANS BALANCE. YOUR HEART IS AS LIGHT AS THE FEATHER OF MA'AT. YOU ARE PURE....

27

No explanation of Kemetic religion, history or philosophy is complete without a discussion of the *Neter* and Concept of *Ma'at*. Ma'at denotes Truth, Justice, Order and Righteousness in all of their purest forms. Ma'at is the ideal of balance: of things working as they should. Ma'at is also the Lady of Truth Who wears a single white ostrich feather on Her head—the symbol of Herself—pure, colorless, light and billowing.

In some Kemetic mythologies, Ma'at is the Daughter of Ra—emanating from the purest light, She comes to put the creations of Ra in balance. In others, She is above and beyond the *Neteru*. In still others, She is the consort of Tehuti, Lord of Wisdom and Knowledge. And at all times She remains an abstract concept, carried by rulers to their people and that which one's heart is weighed against in the final judgment.

Like the Tao (Way) of the ancient Chinese, Ma'at is the force which holds creation together and makes it work like a well-oiled machine. Without Ma'at, chaos reigns unchecked and the ability to create order is forever lost. All is within Her scope: the good and evil, the just and unjust, the understood and the mysterious. There is no thing outside Her vision. Without Ma'at, existence is incomprehensible. She is the absolute against which all particulars are held accountable.

Not surprisingly, Ma'at is difficult to describe. This is not because She is inaccessible; on the contrary, without Her nothing exists. The difficulty lies in Her depth—Her essence is a central mystery of the religion and philosophy of Kemet and would require volumes even to scratch the surface. The best way to know Ma'at is through experience—simply to live, to be and to observe. It becomes very obvious when Ma'at is honored and when She is not and what the consequences are of ignorance of Her Law. Ma'at could be favorably compared with the Eastern concept of *karma* and the Western concept of "common sense." She touches all, encompasses all, affects all, judges all. She is Justice. She is Truth. She is eternal. She is *Ma'at*.

ASET
(ESE, ISIS)

"Golden-tongued Goddess,

Whose voice shall not fail,

skilled to command,

beneficent Aset,

Who rescued Her brother."

—Stele of Amenmose, 18th Dynasty

Foster translation

"I am Aset, Who meets the call for help."

—Coffin Texts 74, Clark translation

"Isis the Divine Mother, Lady of the West.

She gives offerings."

—Papyrus of Nisti-ta-Nebet-Taui, 22nd Dynasty

Piankoff translation

"I invoke you, Great Isis,

ruling in the perfect blackness,

Mistress of the Gods of Heaven from birth."

—Michigan Papyrus 136,

Coptic Period (CE)

Meyer translation

YOU ARE WALKING THROUGH A MARSH. TALL, SHARP GRASSES BOW AT YOUR FEET AND THE MUD SQUISHES UP BETWEEN YOUR TOES. YOU KEEP WALKING UNTIL YOU REACH A CLEARING WHERE YOU BEHOLD A MOTHER SITTING ON A ROCK, SUCKLING HER BABY. SHE LOOKS UP AT YOU WITH THE KINDEST FACE YOU HAVE EVER SEEN. IT IS ALSO A STRONG FACE, STRONG AND SAD. THIS IS ASET, SHE WHO HAS KNOWN GREAT JOYS AND GREAT SORROWS. EVEN NOW, IN THE MARSHES WITH HER SON, SHE SEEMS SADDENED BY SOME LOSS. HER SON IS AS BEAUTIFUL AS SHE IS. SHE MOTIONS WITH HER FREE HAND FOR YOU TO APPROACH....

Most people, even if they know nothing about the religion of Kemet, will know something of the *Neter* Aset, and particularly in Her Greek name of "Isis." This is because Aset, who began in the history of Kemetic religion as a Great *Neter* Who is the wife of Ausar and the Mistress of Magic, became over time one of the most universally recognized and beloved deities ever known by mankind. Her worship lasted longer than the temples dedicated to Her service—and Her image and mythologies were carried far and wide through many lands.

Aset is many things; Lucius Apuleus, in his spiritual experience of Aset, called Her "Isis of Ten Thousand Names." She is wife, mother, lover, sister, daughter and queen. She is a shapeshifter who can become anything from a flying bird to an old wise woman at will. She knows the secret name of Ra, Her father, and therefore holds all of His power, actual and potential, in Her mouth. She is life and resurrection; through her the Great *Neter* Ausar is restored to life long enough to conceive Their love-child, the Avenging Son Heru. On Aset's behalf *Neteru* including Anpu, Tehuti, Nebet Het and Selket lend their aid to find Her dead husband and protect Her from the perils of Her journey.

Aset is patient, kind, wise beyond words and faithful even beyond death; and She is also no stranger to assertiveness or guile. She challenges Her fellow *Neteru* to stand up to Set when He usurps Heru's rightful throne, and through a clever scheme tricks Her father into offering up His name—literally holding Ra's life ransom to make it happen. She is gentle yet unyielding, strong yet kind. Aset's name means "throne," showing Her essence as both the support behind and the enabler of kingship—for without a throne, no Pharaoh is crowned.

Aset has wings to protect Her husband and those who pray to Her in times of need. She has wings to fly to the ends of the world in search of Her beloved and bring Him home again. Along with Her sister Nebet Het (Nephthys) and the *Neteru* Selket (Selkis) and Net (Neith), Aset protects the bodies and shrines of the dead. In later times She acquired the horns-and-sundisk headdress of the Goddess Het-Hert (Hathor), in reflection of the nature of that *Neter*: the Lady of Love, the Divine Mother. In this headdress some people see the moon and the sun—Aset's celestial splendor as Queen of Heaven. In the underworld, She stands beside Her husband Ausar, the Lord of the Dead, to help Him welcome departed souls who have passed their final judgment.

AUSAR
(USIR, OSIRIS)

"I am the fiercely bright one, brother of the fiercely bright one.

I am Osiris, brother of Isis.

My son with His mother Isis saved Me from My enemies,

both male and female, who were doing everything harmful and evil.

....I am Osiris, first-born of the Company,

first-born of the Gods, heir of My father....

I am Osiris, Lord of heads, living of front, vigorous of rear,

vigorous of phallus in the realm of the common folk."

> —*Book of the Dead or Going Forth By Day*
> Utterance 69a, T. G. Allen translation

"O Ausar!

The inundation is coming;

abundance rushes in,

the flood season is coming,

arising from the torrent

issuing from Ausar."

> —*Pyramid Texts* 1944, 2113-2117
> Lamy translation

YOU STAND IN THE CENTER OF A LARGE PLOWED FIELD. THE MOIST BLACK EARTH IS PILED UP IN ROWS AROUND YOU, INDICATING THAT THIS SEASON'S SEEDS HAVE NOT YET BEEN PLANTED. AS YOU WALK THE ROWS, YOU BECOME AWARE OF THE SOUNDS OF HOEING AND A LOW MALE VOICE HUMMING SOME FAMILIAR TUNE. SUDDENLY AUSAR COMES INTO VIEW, BENT OVER A HOLE, CARRYING A WOODEN-HANDLED HOE. HE TURNS TO FACE YOU AND LAUGHS RICHLY. BEFORE YOU KNOW IT YOU ARE STANDING OPPOSITE HIM, HOLDING OUT YOUR HANDS TO RECEIVE A GIFT: A SMALL GREEN SEED. AUSAR NODS AS YOU BEND DOWN AND PLACE THE SEED IN THE HOLE, THEN COVERS IT WITH A FEW SWIPES OF THE HOE. YOU BOTH SIT DOWN TO WATCH IT GROW....

Ausar, like His sister/wife Aset, is a widely-known *Neter* with multiple mythologies. He is alternately the Judge of the Blessed Dead and Lord of the Afterworld, the model of perfect kingship and the Father of Kings. He is also the fertile land of Kemet: the very "black land" the word *kemet* translates into. Through Ausar the yearly inundation of the Nile was secured by Aset and the fields and lands were replenished each spring. The earliest mythologies of Ausar, which always include a cycle of life, death and return, involve Ausar's drowning at the hands of His brother Set (in His role as a storm/desert god). The mythology involving Ausar's dismemberment, reassembly and resurrection is a later myth but is perhaps the best known because it was recorded by Greek historians and was the pervasive mythology in the latter period of Kemet's history.

Ausar's worship began mainly as patron of farmers and the common folk, where the royal clan and nobles were content with the worship of Ra and other kingly *Neteru* such as Heru, Sekhmet and Het-Hert. Ausar's popularity with the masses depended partially on the fact that He represented the inundation by which their agricultural fortunes would rise or fall, and also by the poignant and very humanized mythology surrounding His life, death and continuing reign in the lands of the dead.

Ausar's appeal came from His accessibility and His great love for His people, both in the mythologies as a wise and just king and in His role as beneficent ruler of the lands of the happily departed. Temples rose up at the places where His bodily parts were said to be buried and a tremendous mythological cycle rose up around Ausar that was still being retold (thanks to its recording by Plutarch) centuries after Kemet finally fell to invaders.

In the most ancient texts we have found, Ausar, the local god of the city of Abydos, is an enemy of Ra and a dark, unknown underworld god to whom a dead ruler would

be equated but never subservient. Eventually Ausar was associated with the inundation and instantly became the patron of farmers and those who depended on the land for sustenance. The priest(ess)hood of Ausar, supported by the largely agricultural society, grew in popularity, threatening the power and prestige of the temples of Ra. As time passed Ausar's priest(ess)hood and Ra's priest(ess)hood stopped competing and the

Ausar mythologies were acknowledged in the official state mythology—suddenly rulers, as well, had to appear before Ausar in the Hall of the Double Ma'ati to be judged. Tombs depicted Ausar embracing the dead ruler and his or her *ka*.

The sacred days-long festivals of Ausar, were held with the full sanction of the Great House of Pharaoh. Texts describe them as great celebrations and sacred reenactments allowing the participation of every citizen, and some priests and priestesses in the roles of Ausar, Aset and Their family and friends. The myth of Ausar's imprisonment in a chest and His subsequent death and dismemberment would be related, and the women of the city would go out in mourning with the priestesses representing Aset and Her sister Nebet Het, wailing and searching for the dead Ausar. When all the "pieces" had been found and brought to the temple (a process which could take several days), the divine sisters and Their entourage would return to the temple to sit in mourning with the body, a priest representing Tehuti and a priest representing Anpu. Then, probably related in myth and in drama, Aset with Her magic raised Her husband back to life long enough to conceive Heru, Their son and Ausar's avenger. The next day would begin with a "mock battle" between the followers of Heru and the followers of Set (gangs of townsmen who had divided themselves up, gathered on opposite sides of the city and then marched to the center to confront each other). According to Herodotus, such mock battles were very convincing and could result in serious injuries. When the followers of Heru were declared victorious (as they always were), everyone in the city went to the temple to celebrate the end of the festival and Heru's victory.

Ausar's popularity could not be denied and as a result, He became one of the Greatest *Neteru* and one of the most widely worshipped. In the *Chapters of Going Forth By Day,* the greatest collection of Kemetic religious texts, Ausar is boldly invoked and described: "This is Osiris, son of Nut, greatly feared, held in great awe, to Whom men and gods, the blessed and the dead, have come bowing down. Multitudes have come running to Him; the Dwellers in the Netherworld rejoice before Him."

HERU
(HORUS)

"Who is He?
He to Whom was assigned rule over the Gods
is Horus the son of Isis,
Who was caused to rule in place of His father Osiris."

> —*Book of the Dead or Going Forth By Day*
> Utterance 17b, T. G. Allen translation

"The sky and the Two Lands have been given to Horus.
May I be under the sycamores on the day when He dawns."

> —*Book of the Dead or Going Forth By Day*
> Utterance 181b, T.G. Allen translation

"The fire-child with glittering rays,
dispelling darkness and gloom.
Child increasing in stature and sweet of form,
resting within His Eye."

> —from a teacher's notes, 21st Dynasty
> Erman translation

YOU ARE STANDING IN A GREAT COURTYARD WHEN A GOLDEN CHARIOT, DRAWN BY TWO WHITE HORSES, APPROACHES FROM THE WEST. THE HORSES STOP BEFORE YOU AND YOU GAZE UPON THE DRIVER, BRILLIANT IN BLUE AND GOLD ROBES: THE HAWK-HEADED DIVINE SON, WHO WEARS THE WHITE AND RED CROWNS OF THE TWO LANDS EASILY ON HIS NOBLE HEAD. HE BECKONS FOR YOU TO JOIN HIM IN THE CHARIOT AND YOU CLIMB UP, TREMBLING. AS SOON AS YOU HAVE DONE THIS, HE REACHES FORTH TO STEADY YOU AND THE HORSES SHOOT FORWARD AS THE CHARIOT TAKES OFF QUICKLY AND YOU RIDE WITH HERU ACROSS THE LANDS OF HIS DOMAIN....

It is often difficult to get a grasp on the essence of the *Neter* Heru, for a number of reasons. Most likely is that "Heru" denotes not one, but no less than a dozen different *Neteru*, aspects of Which may or may not be shared with Their other namesakes. The best-known Heru, *Heru-sa-Aset* or "Heru Son of Aset," is only one of a myriad of sky gods Who share the same name.

The one thing the *Neteru* named Heru have in common is Their iconography: a hawk. Some are shown as full hawks; others as hawk-headed men (the sole exception is one depicted as a child holding a finger to His lips, described below). The name *Heru*, which derives from the Kemetic words for "high" or "far off," denotes the sky or heaven, to which Heru is always assigned. Heru is alternately a solar Deity and the swooping hawk which fells its enemies by surprise. Some versions of Heru hold out the symbology of an Eye or Eyes. If two eyes, they are the Sun and Moon (pragmatically, of course: if Heru is the sky, these are His eyes). If one eye, it is the stylized right eye of a hawk or falcon, which offers protection and is a gift to *Neteru* and kings. In religious texts, where a specific liturgical offering is not specified, one often reads "present the Eye of Heru" in its place.

All the Heru-*Neteru* are fierce protectors, of mankind, of other *Neteru*, or of both. For example, Heru-sa-Aset protects His mother Aset and avenges the death of His father Ausar, while Heru-pa-khered (Greek *Harpocrates)*, the child holding a single finger against His lips, is a protector against snakes, scorpions and crocodiles and for the ancient Greeks and modern Ceremonial Magicians is connected with the principle of silence. Heru in some of His earliest forms protects the Two Lands of Kemet, along with Set (in later mythologies these two are cast as irreconcilable enemies, but it is to be remembered that originally They were viewed only as opposing forces who could unite to balance the Two Lands). The depiction of Heru and Set offering life and dominion to a ruler is common on thrones and other royal furniture, and together They hold the ladder to Heaven by which the blessed dead ascend to the Boat of Millions of Years to see Ra. Heru is sometimes consorted with Het-hert, or *Het-heru*, "House of Horus"— a female counterpart of sky to the hawk-god [see the following section on this *Neter* for more information]. Together They were worshipped in the great temple of Dendera.

Heru's connection with solar symbols also resulted in an intimate connection with the royal clan and with Pharaohs in particular. Throughout Kemet's history, Pharaohs are referred to as "the living Heru" and statues depict the Pharaoh being embraced by a hawk, or holding hands with Heru to show their connection. Here, Heru is the son of Ausar (with whom the previous Pharaoh—generally the current Pharaoh's father— would have been identified at death), who carries out His father's will on earth. In some mythologies the two royal *Neteru*, Ra and Heru, are combined to become Ra-Herukhuti (Greek *Ra-Horakhthy)*, "Horus of the Horizon."

NEBET HET
(NEBT-HET, NEPHTHYS)

"I am come to Thee, Nephthys,
I am come to the Evening Barge,
I am come to Thee, True-Is-She-Over-The-Red,
I am come to Thee, She-Who-Remembers-The-*ka*s.
Remember me!"

—*Pyramid Texts of Unas, Utterance 216*
Piankoff translation

"...Nephthys, Divine Sister,
the Eye of Re,
Lady of the Beautiful House.
May She grant that my soul
walks amongst those who are in peace."

—*Papyrus of Ta-Shed-Khonsu,* 22nd Dynasty
Piankoff translation

"I have encircled My brother Osiris;
I have come that I may be thy magical protection.
My protection is around thee, forever;
Thy call has been answered by Ra."

—*Book of the Dead or Going Forth By Day*
Utterance 151c, T. G. Allen translation

YOU STAND IN COMPLETE DARKNESS. SUDDENLY THERE IS A LIGHT SOMEWHERE
IN FRONT OF YOU AND YOU WALK TOWARD IT. IN THE DISTANCE STANDS A
TALL, THIN WOMAN WITH WHAT LOOKS LIKE A CHALICE ON HER HEAD, WHICH
IS ACTUALLY THE HIEROGLYPHIC SYMBOL OF HER NAME: LADY OF THE HOUSE,
NEBET HET. SHE STANDS VERY QUIETLY, WITH HER ARMS HELD OUT, WAITING
FOR YOU....

One of the most enigmatic members of the Kemetic Pantheon is the *Neter* Nebet Het, Whose name is Kemetic for "Lady of the House." She is described in the mythologies as the wife of Set and the sister of both Aset and Ausar, being the last daughter of Ra and Nut to be born. As a manifestation of *Neter* Nebet Het is hard to describe, for she represents one of the greatest mysteries of existence: the journey of death.

With Her great wings, Nebet Het, along with Aset, protects the newly-departed on the journey to the afterworld. In the Pyramid Texts, the long linen bandages of mummies are compared to Her hair. As the "Friend of the Dead," Nebet Het transports the dead Pharaoh on the "evening barge" into the lands of the afterworld. She stands along with Aset behind Ausar in the Hall of the Double Ma'ati, to assist Him in welcoming the virtuous to His blessed fields. Perhaps related to Her intimate connection with death, Nebet Het is also a *Neter* of silence and patience. Wedded to destruction, "true over the red," Nebet Het offers silence and solace, warmth and wings to those who seek peace of any kind.

Nebet Het is also a *Neter* of weeping and sorrow; she mourns the death of Ausar with Aset and wanders the land with Her in the search for His broken body. She stands by as Anpu, Tehuti and Aset prepare Ausar for burial, watching as Aset uses Her magical

voice to stir Ausar's body back to life—just long enough to conceive Heru—then watches silently as He returns to the Land of the Blessed Dead.

Conversely, and to continue the Kemetic philosophy of balance *(ma'at)* in all things, Nebet Het is no one-dimensional *Neter*. She also has a place in the concept of rebirth. Nebet Het is said to be present at childbirth, protecting mothers by standing behind them. She protected Aset's son Heru as well, from the danger of Set. Though Nebet Het to our knowledge never had a temple or priest(ess)hood of Her own in Kemet, She is a *Neter* of great depth and power. It is not by accident that the Great God Anpu is Her son by Her brother Ausar. Though Her essence might not be immediately accessible, Her presence is undeniable—She, like Anpu, is a *Neter* who leads.

SET
(SETH, SUTEKH)

"Who is He?
He is Set.
He is the Great Wild Bull,
He is the soul of Geb."

—The Ancient Egyptian Book of the Dead
R. O. Faulkner translation

"I am Seth, Who causes storms and cloudiness
when I circle about the horizon of the sky."

—Book of the Dead or Going Forth by Day
Utterance 39, T. G. Allen translation

"Thou art conceived, O Set,
as the one whose name is
He-before-Whom-the-sky shakes."

—Pyramid Texts of Unas, Utterance 215
Piankoff translation

"Look here, it was only after he had placed Seth beside Him
that Amon could thunder in the sky."

—The Report of Wenamon
E. F. Wente translation

"I am Seth, greatest in virility among the Ennead,
for I slay the opponent of Ra daily while I am
at the prow of the Bark of the Millions,
whereas not any other God is able to do it."

—The Contendings of Horus and Seth
E. F. Wente translation

THE SAND BELOW YOUR FEET STARTS TO SHIFT AWAY, WHIPPING UP AROUND YOUR ANKLES AS A WIND FROM NOWHERE CUTS ACROSS THE DUNE. YOU REALIZE THE SKY BEHIND YOU IS DARKENING AND ANGRY LIGHTNING BOLTS FLARE IN YOUR DIRECTION. THE SAND STINGS YOUR EYES AND HANDS AS YOU PULL YOUR CLOTHES TOGETHER AND BEGIN TO RUN. THE WIND BECOMES A SMALL GALE AND THE CLOUDS MOVE EVEN CLOSER. THERE IS NOWHERE TO RUN, NO SHELTER. YOUR ESCAPE IS FUTILE. FINALLY THE SANDSTORM IS UPON YOU AND YOU FLING YOURSELF UPON THE DUNE, SHIELDING YOUR FACE AS THE SOUND— THE INCREDIBLE HOWLING SOUND OF SHEETS OF SAND, WIND AND LIGHTNING—ENGULFS EVERY SENSE. ABOVE YOU THE STORM RAGES UNTIL IT FINALLY PASSES AND THE SUN RETURNS, LEAVING YOU TO STAND ALONE IN THE CENTER OF THE SCOURED SURFACE, NO OTHER TRACE OF ITS PASSING IN THE SMOOTH SAND.

OVERCOME, YOU BOW DOWN BEFORE THE MAJESTY OF THE GREAT NETER SET.

Imagine a desert sandstorm, from which there is no shelter. Imagine the sheer strength of a hippopotamus, defending its territory from encroaching humans. Imagine the worst thunderstorm, tornado or hurricane you have lived through. Imagine the sudden fury of an earthquake or the terror of a volcanic eruption. Imagine the original explosion

from which our universe is said to have emerged— the sheer destructive power of that original, one "big bang."

When you can comprehend power without judging it, when you can see that some destruction is necessary chaos, then and only then will you be able to know anything of the *Neter* called Set.

Set, later equated with the Greek Typhon, the serpent of chaos, and even later associated with the Judaeo-Christian Satan, is hardly an embodiment of absolute "evil." Instead He is the essence of masculinity, strength, power and destruction—and specifically the essence of *necessary destruction*. Set is the impetus by which things are destroyed in order for other things to be created. He is the ultimate challenger, daring us to leave behind those things that no longer serve us and to step boldly into the unknown. He is the fractal of chaos theory, the seeming contradictions which finds order in disorder and creation in destruction.

Set is the *Neter* to whom we give our shattered dreams, our lost hopes, our unrealistic goals and our inner failures—to be scoured from existence with the force of a sand-storm. Set's kind of destruction offers freedom from pain, freedom from guilt, a new start. In the mythological metaphor, if Set had not killed His brother Ausar, the Land of the Dead would never have had a champion. Set is part and parcel of our existence, if we only acknowledge Him and honor His contribution.

ANPU
(ANUBIS)

"I have come that I may spread
My protection over you."

—*The Ancient Egyptian Book of the Dead*
R. O. Faulkner translation

"Hail Anpu, come to me.
The High and Mighty,
Chief over the Mysteries
of those in the Underworld;
the Pharaoh of those in Amenti;
the Chief Physician;
the fair son of Ausar,
He whose face is strong among the Gods,
You manifest Yourself in the Underworld
before the hand of Ausar."

—*Leyden Papyrus*
Brier translation

YOU ARE RUNNING THROUGH A GROVE OF DATE PALMS ON A WARM DESERT
EVENING. AT YOUR SIDE, A LONG BLACK DOG WITH TALL EARS IS RUNNING.
YOU RUN FASTER AND HE HAS NO TROUBLE KEEPING UP. HE NIPS PLAYFULLY
AT YOUR HEELS AS YOU RUN AND FALL, LAUGHING, INTO THE SAND. HE LICKS
AT YOUR NOSE, AND THEN DRAWS BACK, EARS PRICKED, A GROWL FORMING IN
HIS THROAT. YOU FEEL VERY SAFE AS YOU KNOW YOU ARE PROTECTED FROM
HARM—AND THAT HE WILL WARN YOU IF YOU STRAY FROM THE PATH. HE IS
FIERCE, YET LOVING AND GENTLE. YOU LOOK AGAIN AND REALIZE YOU HAVE
LOCKED EYES WITH YOUR COMPANION, NOT A DESERT JACKAL BUT THE GREAT
NETER ANPU, FOREMOST OF WESTERNERS, LORD UPON HIS MOUNTAIN....

Originally the primary *Neter* of the afterworld and later the son and protector of Ausar as Lord of the Dead, Anpu serves as the guide of souls in the afterworld, protector of tombs and overseer of the embalming/mummification process. Generally, depictions of Anpu are in reference to funereal rites or show Him in the guise of protecting some other *Neter,* most often Aset, Ausar or Ra. He is depicted as both a canid animal (it is debated whether this animal is a jackal or a dog) and as a canid-headed man. The color attributed to the canid portion of Anpu, however, is never questioned—it is always black, a color associated with death as well as with rebirth—through the fertile Black Land for which Kemet was named.

Anpu is a leader—He guides one's soul to the Hall of the Double Ma'ati for judgment; and yet He is also a follower—quietly behind a person, Anpu will prevent him or her from straying from the intended destination by fending off attackers or by nudging the person in the right direction. Anpu oversees the preparations of the dead for interment, assuring their perfection. He also is the only *Neter* to touch the scales in the Hall of the Double Ma'ati, assuring the judged that his or her heart will be justly weighed against Ma'at's feather of truth, making sure the balance is true as the baboon of Tehuti and the dead person's *ka* look on. Without Anpu's expert guidance and care, the underworld would become a bewildering maze, from which it would be difficult, if not impossible, to emerge. Anpu leads us to both His mothers: to Nebet Het, the patient, silent Friend and Comforter of the Dead; and to Aset, His foster mother, the Great *Neter* of Magic and Love. He leads us to His father Ausar, Judge of the Living and the Dead, the One Who rises up though He was killed.

When lost in darkness, look for the sharp eyes of a jackal, and know you are never truly alone as long as Anpu exists to show the way.

⟨hieroglyphs⟩ HET-HERT ⟨hieroglyph⟩
(HET HERET, HATHOR)

"I praise the Golden Goddess,
I exalt Her Majesty,
I raise high the Lady of Heaven,
I make praise for Hathor,
and chants for My Mistress."

— *"Songs of Extreme Happiness,"* fifth stanza
The Chester Beatty Love Songs
fifth stanza

"After a long space, Hathor, the Lady of the Southern Sycamore,
came and stood before Her father, the Master of the Universe,
and She uncovered Her nakedness before His face.
And He laughed at Her."

—*The Contendings of Horus and Seth*
Chester Beatty Papyrus #1
Gardiner translation

"Hathor, Lady of the West, Thou of the starboard side,
Lady of the Sacred Land, Eye of Ra in His forehead,
beautiful of face in the Bark of Millions of Years,
seat of rest for the doer of righteousness,
ferryboat of the favored ones,
Whose place it is to provide the great *neshmet* boat
to take the righteous across."

—*Book of the Dead or Going Forth By Day*
Utterance 186, T. G. Allen translation

ENTER THE TEMPLE OF HET-HERT. THERE ARE MANY WOMEN WALKING
AROUND YOU, WOMEN WITH CHILDREN, YOUNG WOMEN, PRIESTESSES,
WIVES, MOTHERS, LOVERS. THEY BOW AND SMILE AS YOU PASS, ON YOUR

WAY TO THE LADY'S SHRINE. YOU PASS THE HOUSE OF BIRTH, WHERE PREGNANT WOMEN GO TO HAVE THEIR CHILDREN UNDER THE WATCHFUL EYE OF THE NE-TER AND HER MIDWIFE HANDMAIDENS. AROUND A BEND, YOU FIND YOU HAVE REACHED THE SHRINE AND YOU ENTER. SHE IS WAITING FOR YOU: THE COW, THE WOMAN WITH A SISTRUM, THE GREAT QUEEN….

Predynastic Nile peoples saw in the cow a perfect symbol of motherhood: she was gentle and patient and provided sustenance in the form of milk to her children. As a result, they associated the heavens with a "celestial cow," which sent sustenance in the form of rain and whose four legs marked the ends of the earth. In time this celestial bovine was equated with the *Neter* Het-hert, or "House of Heru."

It makes sense for the heaven to be the House of Heru—as Heru is primarily a solar Deity and a great soaring hawk. Het-hert, therefore, is the Kemetic Queen of Heaven, *Neter* of plenty. She is also the Lady of the West, west being the direction of the setting sun, where the blessed dead reside. For its gentle shade and sweet perfume, the sycamore tree also was associated with Her, as well as the ritual rattle held only by priestesses, called a *sistrum.*

Het-hert is a Great Mother Goddess, the highest archetype of motherhood, of beauty and of femininity. Her temples, at least in Kemet's later periods, were inhabited by women; every Queen of Kemet was associated with Het-hert either as Her priestess or as Her living embodiment on earth or as both. Her headdress, a solar disk surmounted by cow's horns, was a popular headdress for queens and priestesses and eventually was also attributed to the *Neter* Aset, another Lady of the West and Queen of Heaven with Whom Het-hert has much in common.

Het-hert is a Daughter of Ra; in some mythologies an angry Het-hert is equated with Sekhmet as *Neter* of Plague and Destruction. Het-hert as a sacred cow waited in a mountain in the west for the Boat of Millions of Years so that She could receive Her father at sunset. Het-hert's worship was associated with dancing and perfumes and sweet music; in fact, along with the Great *Neter* Bast, Het-hert can be said to be the *Neter* of music and dance. Her head, adorned with bovine ears, was set atop columns in many temples and homes, as well as a decoration on the handles of sacred sistra and mirrors.

She is the *Neter* of Love in every facet; Her type and attributes later were given over to the Greek Goddess Aphrodite and to a composite *Neter*, Aset-Het-hert, Whose worship was enjoyed in Mediterranean lands beyond Kemet and Greece. Het-hert is also a *Neter* of happiness and good humor; a myth relates that one day when Ra was unhappy, Het-hert took off Her clothing and danced naked around the throne room until He cheered up.

Het-hert is the *Neter* who gives nourishment; the milk of kindness is Her gift. (In fact, milk is used as a sacred beverage in Her worship.)

If love is all we need, then Het-Hert is the *Neter* the world needs to seek.

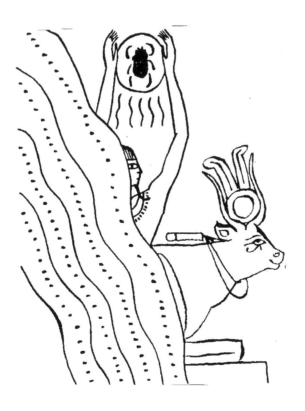

PTAH
(PTAH-TENEN)

"His beauty is in every body.

Ptah has done this with His own hands, to rejoice His heart.

The pools are freshly filled with water,

the earth brims over with love for Him."

—from a song inscribed in the tomb
of Neb-Amen, Thebes (18th Dynasty)

"Ptah art Thou, for Thou fashionest Thy body.

O God who bore Himself and was not born,

as Ra rising in the sky of eternity,

the necropolis of the favored ones,

join the august initiates of the God's domain

and go forth with Them to see Thy beauty when Thou risest.

In the evening Thou hast traversed Thy mother the Nether Sky.

While Thou directest Thy face toward the west,

my arms are raised in praise at Thy setting in life,

for Thou art the maker of eternity,

adored when Thou settest in the deep.

I fix Thee in my heart, unwearying One,

more divine than all the other Gods."

—*Book of the Dead or Coming Forth By Day*
Utterance 15d, T. G. Allen translation

"Homage to Thee, Ptah-Tenen, Thou Great God, Whose form is hidden!

Thou openest Thy soul and Thou wakest in peace,

O Father of the Fathers of all the Gods,

Thou Disk of Heaven!

Thou illuminatest it with Thy two eyes,

and Thou lightest up the earth with Thy brilliant rays in peace."

—*Hymn to Ptah-Tenen,* 20th or 21st Dynasty

Lepsius translation

YOU ARE STANDING IN A GREAT COURTYARD BEFORE A TEMPLE THAT IS BEING BUILT. MANY WORKERS ARE ON WOODEN SCAFFOLDS, LIFTING HUGE STONES INTO PLACE, CARRYING AND PAINTING, WHILE THE FOREMEN SHOUT UP INSTRUCTIONS FROM THE GROUND AND THE HAMMERS AND CHISELS RING OUT. MANY FOREMEN HAVE GATHERED AROUND ONE PERSON STANDING AT THE END OF THE COURTYARD. YOU APPROACH AND SEE THAT THEY ARE STANDING AROUND THE GREAT NETER PTAH, WHO HOLDS THE BLUEPRINT FOR THE FINISHED TEMPLE IN HIS HANDS, POINTING OUT TO THE WORKERS HOW IT WILL LOOK WHEN COMPLETED. SUDDENLY HE STOPS TALKING TO THEM AND ACKNOWLEDGES YOUR PRESENCE, DRAWING YOU INTO THEIR CIRCLE....

Ptah is often characterized by scholars as the only *Neter* to have an "abstract" quality in the fashion of later divinities like the Judeo-Christian "God." This is not true—solar *Neteru* including Tem and Amen have the same abstract, "hidden" quality; some primeval *Neteru,* such as the Ogdoad (eight divinities) of Hermopolis, are characterized by having no easily accessible aspects whatsoever; and in the eyes of the people of Kemet,

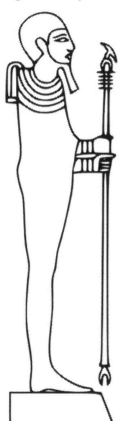

all *Neteru* are essentially "hidden" and "unknowable." Ptah does have the distinction of being one of the most widely-worshipped of the *Neteru* by the people of Kemet across its history—He was the primary *Neter* and creator-god of the city of Memphis (known in Kemet as *Het ka Ptah,* or "House of the *ka* of Ptah"), for its entire history— nearly 4,000 years.

The Great *Neter* Ptah is the immanent creator from Whom all other *Neteru* issued in creation (in the same fashion as Tem and Amen are in other mythologies) and the patron of craftsmen and those who create. The temples of Ptah were training grounds for sculptors, painters and craftsmen of all types. With the exception of writing, all the plastic, creative arts are attributed to Ptah. His highest priest(ess) in Kemet was known as "master builder" or "master craftsman," a title which filtered down through history to be associated with the Masonic fraternal orders. The Greeks equated Ptah with Hephaestos and held Him in great regard.

Ptah's popularity never waned in Kemet, even during the New Kingdom, when the national capital moved from Memphis to Thebes (in Kemetic, *Uaset)* and the local *Neter* Amen was touted as Sole Creator and King of the *Neteru.* New Kingdom and later Pharaohs held festivals in which they would pay homage to both the Hidden Lord and the Great *Neter* of Memphis. The sacred image of Amen in Thebes would be taken in procession to "visit" Ptah of Memphis, and vice versa.

Ptah is almost always portrayed as a mummified man wearing a tight-fitting cap and a false beard signifying divinity, holding the symbols of royalty, power, life and stability in His unwrapped hands. Sometimes, as Ptah-Tenen, He is portrayed as a tall, strong man wearing the *nemes* (striped, long headcloth) of a Pharaoh. His consort is the Great Goddess Sekhmet, Who in Her aspect as a destroyer is the complementary opposite of Ptah as creator; together They are attributed with two sons: Nefer-Tem, a *Neter* of beauty and perfume, and Imhotep, a *Neter* of healing and knowledge.

A surviving inscription of Ptah named the Shabaqa Stone (because of its creation during the reign of Pharaoh Shabaqa, (25th Dynasty, c710 BCE), describes Ptah in a fashion that caused early archaeologists to make comparisons to the Judeo-Christian concept of divinity. In the Shabaqa inscription, which states that it is a copy of an original document dating many centuries before Shabaqa but found in such a decayed state that the Pharaoh ordered it cut into stone for preservation, Ptah is described as an immanent, unknowable quality; a power beyond human comprehension that created all that exists from Himself through His voice (equated with the Great *Neter* Tehuti) and directed by the desires of His heart (equated with the Great *Neter* Heru). Together, this "trinity" of Mind (Ptah), Heart (Heru) and Voice (Tehuti) work to bring all creation into existence. To archaeologists who had thought the people of Kemet primitive and incapable of abstract reasoning, especially in a religious sense, the discovery of the Shabaqa Stone was a shock. It meant that modern religion did not have a monopoly on abstract philosophy—and even more shockingly, as the original the Shabaqa Stone had been copied from predated the Hebrews' sojourn in Kemet, that the Kemetic philosophy surrounding Ptah might actually have *influenced* Hebraic conceptions of divinity and therefore current Judaeo-Christian ideas of the nature of the Divine.

The finding of the Shabaqa Stone and the translation of its script began a new era in scholars' thinking on the nature of Ptah, and all the *Neteru*. When you begin to work with Them, you will learn that at the heart of each and every *Neter* is an inherent mystery. This inscription, and through it the Great *Neter* Ptah, are the first indicators of the need for unbiased thought on the religion of Kemet by modern scholars—proof that this "primitive" Pagan religion is hardly primitive at all.

SEKHMET
(SACHMIS)

"I make petition, so that You may hear, O Person of Gold!

I make supplication that Your heart be turned to me!

Hail to You, Lady of Plague,

Sekhmet the Great, Lady to the Limit!

Extolled one upon Your father, eldest one before Her maker,

Foremost of place in the Boat of Millions of Years,

free-striding in the cabin!

It is Your arms which give light,

Your rays which illumine the Two Lands.

The Two Banks are under Your counsel.

The sunfolk are Your flock!"

—Tomb of Senet, Middle Kingdom
Parkinson translation

"How strong She is! Without contender,

She honors Her name as Queen of the Cities.

Sharp-sighted, keen as God's protector, Right Eye of Ra,

disciple facing Her Lord, bright with the Glory of God,

wise upon Her high throne,

She is Most Holy of Places,

a mecca the world cannot parallel."

—*Leyden Hymn 10*, 19th Dynasty
Foster translation

YOU ARE IN A FIELD OF TALL WAVING GRASSES. IN THE DISTANCE, YOU WATCH A HERD OF ANTELOPE, GIRAFFES AND SOME ZEBRA GRAZE AND REST. BEHIND YOU THERE IS A RUSTLE IN THE GRASS AND THEN A HUGE LIONESS COMES INTO VIEW. SHE REGARDS YOU WITH LARGE, GOLDEN EYES THAT SEEM TO KNOW YOU INSIDE OUT. SHE IS NOT AFRAID OF YOUR PRESENCE, NOR YOU OF HERS. YOU REALIZE THIS IS NO ORDINARY LIONESS AND SHE MOMENTARILY TRANSFORMS INTO

HER HALF-HUMAN, HALF-LIONESS FORM BEFORE YOU: SEKHMET, THE LADY IN
RED. THEN, QUICKLY REVERTING TO LIONESS FORM, SHE PUSHES BEYOND YOU
AND BIDS YOU FOLLOW. THE HUNT IS ON....

Sekhmet is certainly not a *Neter* to be taken lightly. Portrayed as a lioness-headed woman or as a full lioness, She is the Daughter of Ra, His protector and avenger, Who goes
out into the world to ward off Ra's enemies. She is the Lady in Red, a powerful female
Whose vengeance is terrible and swift, a great mother Who shields Her children from
all adversity with the fierce love of a lioness.

Sekhmet is one of the oldest *Neteru* known to Kemet, a strong
mother, a protector and an earth *Neter.* Her priest(ess)hood
served the people of Kemet as trained surgeons and doctors.
Sekhmet, Whose name is derived from *sekhem,* the Kemetic word
for "power" or "might," was held in honor by Pharaohs and
countryfolk alike as protector of the innocent and avenger of the
wronged. Her strength was legendary and She was invoked in all
things involving healing and to turn back plagues and infections.

Like a lioness, Sekhmet is a huntress—but an *appropriate* huntress, who hunts only for food and then brings it back to share
with the rest of the pride. This concept of "appropriate action" is
central to the essence of Sekhmet—She acts only where appropriate, in appropriate fashion. Her destructive vengeance is never
chaotic or random; it is always what is necessary and it is always
just enough. In this respect She resembles the Great *Neter* Set, though Her jurisdiction
is not over destruction *per se* as much as the removal of threats and the punishment of
wrongdoing. In Memphis Sekhmet was held to be the wife of Ptah, in a relationship of
opposites—creation and destruction, complementing each other.

The greatest myth about Sekhmet revolves around Her near-destruction of humankind.
In the beginning of the myth, Ra is angered by the lawlessness of His children on earth
and their refusal to uphold righteousness and honor Him. After consulting with the
rest of the *Neteru,* Ra decides to send forth His "eye," Sekhmet, to punish the wrongdo-
ers. Sekhmet repels an army sent against Her, killing anyone who attacks Her as She is

carrying out Her father's wishes; then going to rest for the night and giving the army an opportunity to leave (the appropriate action). When, in the morning, Sekhmet learns the army still stands against Her, She becomes enraged and in Her bloodlust begins to slaughter indiscriminately. Ra realizes that if She is not stopped, humankind will be destroyed. He summons Sekhmet's handmaidens to gather beer and mandrakes and orders them to pour it out over a field until they create a deep red lake. Sekhmet stumbles upon the lake of red liquid, and, thinking it to be blood, drinks until She is so drunk She falls asleep and Her anger passes, and humanity is saved. (In some versions of the myth, Tehuti is then dispatched to bring the exhausted *Neter* back to Ra's palace.) In honor of this myth, the yearly festival of Sekhmet involved the preparation and drinking of quantities of red beer—as many jars full as there were priest(ess)es to share it.

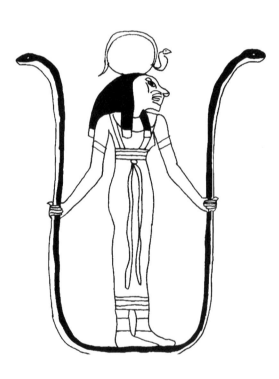

BAST
(UBASTET, PASHT)

"....Bastet, Who protects the Two Lands."

—*The Loyalist Instruction of Sehetepibre*
Georges Pozener translation

"Hail to Thee....Eye of Re, Mistress of the Gods, plume-wearer....

Sole one superior to Her father, to whom no gods can become superior,

Great of magic in the Bark of Millions of Years,

Sacred one dawning in the seat of silence....strife and peace are in Thy grasp.

....Praise to Thee, Who art stronger than the gods; joy to Thee."

—*Book of the Dead or Going Forth By Day*
Utterance 164, T. G. Allen translation

YOU STAND OUTSIDE THE GATE OF A GREAT TEMPLE. AROUND YOUR FEET ARE HUNDREDS AND THOUSANDS OF CATS....CATS OF ALL COLORS AND BREEDS, MALE AND FEMALE, KITTENS AND ANCIENT CATS WHOSE WHISKERS ARE BRITTLE. THEY CALL OUT AND SING TO YOU. IN THE DISTANCE, YOU HEAR MUSIC, THE SHAKING OF A SISTRUM AND A HARP, ALONG WITH LAUGHTER AND THE SOUNDS OF DANCING DRUMS. AT THE BACK OF YOUR NECK YOU FEEL THE BRUSH OF A WHISKER AND WARM BREATH AND TURN TO FIND BAST STANDING BEHIND YOU, SMILING WITH HUGE GREEN EYES. SHE LAUGHS SENSUALLY AT YOUR SURPRISE, THEN REACHES DOWN AND PICKS UP A KITTEN TO PET IT, DRAWING CLOSER....

Ironically, one of the most popular *Neteru* in Kemetic history is one of the most difficult to find information on. Bast (sometimes called *Bastet)* is one of the oldest *Neteru* on record; we have an inscription dating Her back to the Second Dynasty as "Bast, Lady of the Life of the Two Lands" *(Bast Nebet Ankh-taui)*. She was originally depicted as a lion-headed woman and associated with divine vengeance, warfare and the protection of the Pharaoh; Her visage was cut into shields and Her temple visited before battles. As Kemet progressed, much of Her vengeful (lion-like) nature was downplayed to be replaced with the more benign (cat-like) attributes of fertility and contentment, perhaps somehow echoing the evolution of her animal symbol from a wild lioness to that of a domesticated cat. However this evolution was intended, it did not change Bast's fundamental nature so much as the people of Kemet's response to it—the people of Kemet still knew and remembered Who Bast was. Unfortunately, later societies have not had as easy a time dealing with seeming contradictions and lack of duality in conceptions of Deity. As a result, modern scholars often have a difficult time separating the essences of Bast from those of Sekhmet (also a lioness-Goddess and Daughter of Ra), and often set them together as the same divinity in a dichotomy of "nice kitty/big bad lioness." This is not only incorrect, but devalues the worth of the multifaceted approach the religion of Kemet offers to the *Neteru*. There was a composite *Neter* known as *Sekhmet-Bast-Ra,* but this *Neter* was a true composite: the union of the individual *Neteru* did not negate Their individualities in a seeming paradox which is a central issue of Kemetic philosophy, called by archaeologist Erik Hornung the concept of "the one and the many."

Bast's city, Per-Bast (known to the Greeks as *Bubastis* and listed in the Old Testament of the Bible as *Pi-beseth),* had at its center a moat made by two streams of the Nile, enclosing a red granite temple wall with a grove of trees inside instead of the usual closed shrine, hypostyle hall and courtyard. The temple was home to a large number of cats, both in life and as a repository for their remains (interestingly enough, according to Naville, most of the feline remains found at Per-Bast were incinerated, as if cremated, instead of mummified as in other temple cemeteries). In fact, cats of all sorts were associated with Bast throughout Kemet's history, and as Her image evolved into that of a cat-headed woman, She was also depicted as a complete cat (close to our domesticated cat, but a little bit larger and having a striped tail) with the Eye of Ra around its neck. The color green and the precious stone malachite (for which the *nome* or precinct of Per-Bast was known) are associated with Bast, as are the *sistrum* used in Het-hert's worship, music and dancing.

Bast is a protective *Neter* as well as the *Neter* of joy and fertility. In later times Her festivals were attended by vast crowds (perhaps up to 100,000 women, men and children), involving orgiastic parties and boat processions. Her festivals were so popular that a Greek historian, Herodotus, chose the festivals of Bast to write about in his historical records as an example of Kemet's public rituals. At any given time Bast was one of the most widely worshipped *Neteru* among the common people; Her honor in the state religion rose and fell with the popularity of other *Neteru* until the 22nd and 23rd Dynasties, when Per-Bast became the national capital along with Thebes, Bast became state Goddess and was officially worshipped by all Kemet. Temple ruins at Per-Bast depict great festivals held by Pharaoh Osorkon II under Her watchful eye, and several Pharaohs of that period bore Her name as part of their coronation names (e.g., Petubast, Sibast).

Bast is the Lady of Pleasure and Sexuality, similar to Het-Hert (In some mythologies, Bast, Sekhmet, Mut and Aset are all said to be aspects of Het-hert). She is sometimes called the "soul of Aset," probably a pun on Her name in relation to Her protective and magical powers. Bast was associated with both the sun (as a Daughter of Ra) and with the moon (in later periods, the fact that cats' eyes glow in the dark was attributed to the moon somehow being "kept" in them). In the Pyramid Texts Bast is called "First Daughter of Tem" and is in that respect a direct reflection of the creative essence—the life that dances forth from creation. Her name, which means "to tear" or "to rend," implies fierceness but is yet tempered with frivolity, and She displays happiness interspersed with seriousness, being able to work and play in balance. Her influence on one's life is immediate and, like that of any other of the *Neteru,* cannot be ignored; and also like the rest of Them, Her love and Her joy know no bounds.

THIS WAS ITS UNFOLDING,
FROM BEGINNING TO END,
AS FOUND IN WRITING.

FOR FURTHER READING

Allen, T.G., trans. *The Book of the Dead or Going Forth By Day: Ideas of the Ancient Egyptians concerning the hereafter as expressed in their own terms.* Oriental Institute of the University of Chicago, Studies in Ancient Oriental Civilization #37, 1974. ISBN 226-6240-2.

> This book is the best direct translation currently available of the different parts of
> the religious texts collectively called "Book of the Dead." Difficult to find, but
> highly recommended.

Barrett, Clive. *The Egyptian Gods and Goddesses.* Aquarian/Thorsons (HarperCollins), 1991. ISBN 0-85030-929-8.

> A "New Age" type discussion of the *Neteru*, but well-documented and full of perhaps
> the most beautiful illustrations I have ever seen. An aside: I strongly disagree with his equation
> of the Goddesses Nut and Net (Neith) as the same *Neter*.

Breasted, James Henry. *Development of Religion and Thought in Ancient Egypt.* New York, 1912.

> Unfortunately out of print at this writing, this book is a transcription of a number
> of lectures J.H. Breasted, founder of the Oriental Institute for the study of Ancient
> Near Eastern history, philosophy and religion, offered his students on the subject of
> Kemetic religion. It is one of the most concise and accurate (i.e., non-biased) treatises
> on the subject—unlike many of his early 20th Century colleagues, Breasted is able to
> put aside his Western/Christian biases to examine Kemetic thought in its own
> perspective. Highly recommended.

Ellis, Normandi, transl. *Awakening Osiris: The Egyptian Book of the Dead.* Phanes Press, 1988. ISBN 0-933999-74-7.

> A modern-English, free interpretation based on Sir E.A. Wallis Budge's translations
> of differing *Books of the Dead.* Simply beautiful. The book is also available as a tape
> recording (two audiotapes) read by Jean Houston. Very highly recommended.

Faulkner, R.O., trans. *The Ancient Egyptian Book of the Dead.* University of Texas Press, Austin, 1990. ISBN 0-292-70425-9.

> Another direct translation of the *Book of the Dead,* this one containing full-color reproductions from different papyri illustrating the different chapters. Easier to read than the Allen translation because of its chapter-and-paragraph layout. Highly recommended.

ibid. *The Ancient Egyptian Coffin Texts.* Warminster: Aris & Phillips, 1978

> A volumes-long look at the *Coffin Texts,* precursors to the *Book of the Dead.*

ibid. *The Ancient Egyptian Pyramid Texts.* Warminster: Aris & Phillips.

> Before the *Book of the Dead* and the *Coffin Texts,* there were the *Pyramid Texts,* a set of funereal formulas for the transition of a dead ruler to the afterworld used in the Old Kingdom. These are some of Kemet's oldest surviving religious texts.

Foster, John L., trans. *Echoes of Egyptian Voices: An Anthology of Ancient Egyptian Poetry.* University of Oklahoma Series in Classical Culture Volume 12, 1992. ISBN 0-8061-2411-3.

> A collection of poetry including love songs, hymns and wisdom literature spanning the entire history of Kemet. Highly recommended, but unfortunately currently out of print.

Gardiner, Sir Alan. *Egyptian Grammar: Being An Introduction to the Study of Hieroglyphs.* Griffith Institute, Ashmolean Museum, Oxford, 1957 (Third ed. 1988). ISBN 0-900416-35-1.

> Used as a textbook in Egyptology courses, Gardiner's book remains the authority on learning to write and read hieroglyphs (Old through Middle Kingdom). Very expensive (at least $65 at this writing) but essential for the serious student of Kemetic language.

Hart, George. *A Dictionary of Egyptian Gods and Goddesses.* Routledge, 1986.
ISBN 0-415-05909-7.

> An encyclopedic look at the *Neteru* in alphabetical order.

Hornung, Erik; translated by John Baines. *Conceptions of God in Ancient Egypt: The One and The Many.* Cornell University Press, 1982. ISBN 0-8014-1223-4.

> A thought-provoking look at the philosophy behind Kemetic religion, the Kemetic
> concept of Deity and its contribution to the development of other world religions
> and philosophies. Very highly recommended.

Lichtheim, Miriam, transl. *Ancient Egyptian Literature.* (3 volumes). University of California Press, 1976. ISBN 0-520-03615-8.

> A collection of Kemetic literature arranged chronologically in three volumes: The Old
> and Middle Kingdoms, The New Kingdom and the Late Period and beyond. Covers
> most of the well-known Kemetic religious and philosophical texts and includes poetry,
> short stories and instructional literature. Highly recommended.

Naville, Edouard. *Bubastis, 1887-1889.* Eighth Memoir of the Egypt Exploration Fund, 1891.

> The original archaeological memoirs from the excavations of Per-Bast, the City of Bast.
> Very rare. Full of detailed drawings and descriptions of Per-Bast's temple precinct.

ibid. *The Festival Hall of Osorkon II in the Great Temple of Bubastis, 1887-1889.* Tenth Memoir of the Egypt Exploration Fund, 1892.

> The second part of Naville's excavation memoirs, detailing the *heb-sed* or rejuvenation festival of
> Pharaoh Osorkon II, ruler during the (Bubastite) 22nd Dynasty. Also
> very rare.

Parker, R.A. *The Calendars of Ancient Egypt.* Oriental Institute of the University of Chicago, 1950.

> A detailed comparison of different papyri and texts to complete a calendar of ancient Kemet, with festivals, etc.

Parkinson, R.B. *Voices from Ancient Egypt: An Anthology of Middle Kingdom Writings.* University of Oklahoma Press, 1991. ISBN 0-8061-2362-1.

> A collection of writings from Kemet's Middle Kingdom, including hymns, short stories, letters (even "hate mail"!) and magical formulas. An interesting look at one period of Kemet's history from its own literature, with good interpretations alongside the texts. Highly recommended.

Piankoff, A. *Mythological Papyri.* Bollingen Series, Egyptian Religious Texts and Representations, 1957.

> A collection of Late Period funereal papyri from a cache of tombs for priests and priestesses of the *Neter* Amen-Ra. A book with a transcription of hieroglyphs and their English translation is accompanied by more than 30 full reproductions of the papyri being discussed, several in color. Very rare but useful information regarding different *Neteru* and the afterworld.

ibid. *The Pyramid Texts of Unas.* Bollingen Series, Egyptian Religious Texts and Representations, 1957.

> One volume in a set of reproductions/translations of Kemetic texts and tomb murals, the *Pyramid Texts of Unas* are perhaps the best known and most complete of the *Pyramid Texts.* Highly recommended as it is one of the earliest looks at Kemetic religion.

Schafer, Byron E., ed. *Religion in Ancient Egypt: Gods, Myths and Personal Practice.* Cornell University Press, 1991. ISBN 0-8014-2550-6.

> A collection of scholarly papers on Kemetic religion, sacred kingship and perceptions of Deity.

Simpson, William Kelly, ed. *The Literature of Ancient Egypt: An Anthology of Stories, Instruction and Poetry.* Yale University Press, 1972. ISBN 0-300-01711-1.

> Another anthology of Kemetic texts, collected from different Egyptologists'
> translations.

Versluis, Arthur. *The Egyptian Mysteries.* Arkana, 1988. ISBN 1-85063-087-9.

> A scholarly dissertation on the nature of Kemetic religion and religious philosophy,
> comparing it to other Occidental and Oriental religious systems including Buddhism, Hinduism
> and the Pagan religion of Greece. I disagree with Versluis' characterization
> of Set (whom he equates with Typhon) but else this is a very informative, if complex,
> book. Recommended for the student with some familiarity with comparative religion, Greek and
> Oriental philosophy. Currently out of print.

GLOSSARY

BENNU

The same as the Greek "phoenix," or the bird of the sun-god (Ra), which rose from the primeval hill at the creation. From the Kemetic *weben*, "to shine."

BOOK OF THE DEAD/CHAPTERS OF GOING FORTH BY DAY

A collection of funereal texts popular from the end of the Middle Kingdom forward, basically a papyrus form of the previous era's *Coffin Texts*. Available to any member of society who could afford to have a copy made for him or herself, the *Chapters of Going Forth By Day* are a basic reflection of Kemetic beliefs about the afterworld and the soul's progress through it.

COFFIN TEXTS

A collection of funereal texts written directly onto the coffins and sarcophagi of noble-men and women from the Middle Kingdom. These were a carryover from the Old Kingdom's *Pyramid Texts,* which provided for safe passage of the ruler through the afterworld.

EGYPT

The Greek name for the land of Kemet, thought to be derived from *Het-ka-Ptah*, the Ke-metic name for the longtime state capital of Memphis.

EYE OF HERU

A symbolic stylized hawk's eye (usually the right eye) associated with protection and the presentation of gifts; also associated with the *Neter* Heru as the orb of the sun.

EYE OF RA

The Eye of Ra can be either the same as the *Eye of Heru* (see above entry), or is used as a title for a protectress or vengeful *Neter* associated with Ra. Sekhmet, Bast and Buto/Wadjet are associated with/called "Eye of Ra" in differing texts throughout Kemetic history, as occasionally is the *Neter* Het-hert.

HALL OF THE DOUBLE MA'ATI

"Hall of the Two Truths," the judgment hall where one's heart is weighed against Ma'at's feather of truth by Anpu, as Tehuti records the result. Those who pass are declared "pure" and led by Heru to His Father Ausar. Those who do not are fed to *Ammit,* a *Neter* depicted as part lion, part crocodile and part hippopotamus, whose purpose is to utterly destroy wickedness.

HEM NETER

"Servant of *Neter,*" the commonest title of an ordained priest. Feminine form *Hem(e)t Neter* or Handmaiden (ordained priestess) of *Neter.* Sometimes the word *Neter* is replaced with the name of the divinity served: for example, *Hem Khepera* or *Hem(e)t Ptah.*

HET-KA-PTAH

"House of the *ka* of Ptah," the Kemetic name for the city and longtime national capital of Memphis.

HYPOSTYLE HALL

A hall characterized by its layout: a rectangular space with a long passageway between a great number of columns holding up the roof. For example, the hypostyle hall in the temple of Amen-Ra at Karnak had more than 100 columns.

KA

The spiritual "double" or Higher Self of a person, a *ka* is the reflection of one's personal *Neter* and one attempts to "feed" his or her own *ka* with good deeds and truth; i.e., with Ma'at. In worship, ritual gifts and incense feed the *kas* of the *Neteru.*

KEMET

"Black Land," the name the peoples who lived on the banks of the river Nile north from the Third Cataract to the Mediterranean gave to their country.

KHER-HEB

"Lector-priest/ess," the title given to the Servant or Handmaiden who recites the liturgy and magical formulae in temple. In antiquity, sometimes equated with the "learned" members of the priest(ess)hood, who could read hieroglyphs and therefore "knew the words of power."

MA'AT
The *Neter* and abstract concept of truth, justice and order.

METU NETER
"Words of the God(s)," or sacred hieroglyphic writing.

NETERU (NEDJERU)
"Powers" or "Divinities," the Kemetic term for God/dess.

NEMES
A headcloth, generally striped, worn by Kemetic men and especially the Pharaoh. (Female pharaohs, such as Hatshepsut, also wore the *nemes*.)

NOME
A Greek term used to denote the different "states" or provinces of Kemet. There were 42 different nomes, distributed equally between Upper and Lower Kemet.

OBELISK
A tall square column with a pyramid atop it, often covered with inscriptions, generally erected at the front of a temple in honor of a *Neter*.

ORISHA
"Powers," the name for divinities in the indigenous African religion of Yoruba, and also in an Afro-Caribbean derivative, the religion of Santer"a.

PYLON
A formal gateway within a temple. Pylons were made of bricks and often covered with scenes having to do with the life and exploits of the ruler(s) who built them; some surviving temple pylons are more than 60 feet high.

PYRAMID

A building formed in the shape of a geometric pyramid for the housing of royal remains. Pyramids were built later in Kemet's history but the best-known and largest examples (e.g., Great Pyramid of Khufu, Khafre Pyramid, Bent Pyramid, Step Pyramid etc.) were built during Kemet's first four dynasties in the Old Kingdom. Contrary to current New Age characterizations, pyramids are *not* temples and were never used as such by the Kemetic people; each pyramid has a temple for the ruler buried within it at its front entrance (outside and in front of it, a separate structure). The pyramid shape is thought to evoke the *benben,* or the primeval hill/mountain of creation from which the *Bennu* (see above entry) emerged.

PYRAMID TEXTS

A collection of funereal texts provided for the dead rulers in their pyramid tombs in the Old Kingdom. They are the oldest surviving religious texts of Kemet.

SENET

A Kemetic board-game consisting of moving a number of pieces around a board with squares, popular among the noble class.

SESH-PER-ANKH

"Scribe of the House of Life," the title of a priest(ess) whose temple duty is to record temple occurrences, oracles received from the *Neteru,* etc. The *sesh-per-ankh* in antiquity was also in charge of the temple libraries and a holder of great knowledge. Some archaeologists connect the *sesh-per-ankh* with the figure of the Kemetic "magician," a learned person/priest/doctor, who had intimate knowledge of religious and magical texts and was consulted by the priest(ess)hood and common folk for simple charms and divinations, spellcraft and medical treatment.

SHABAQA STONE

An inscription dating from the reign of Pharaoh Shabaqa (25th Dynasty, c 710 BCE), to record an earlier, worm-eaten papyrus concerning a sacred drama of the coronation of the *Neter* Heru, but most importantly, the mythology of the *Neter* Ptah and the creation of the world, cited by modern scholars as evidence of a deeply spiritual and abstract religious philosophy in Kemet.

SISTRUM

A ritual percussion instrument consisting of a long loop of metal suspended from a metal or wooden handle, upon which are attached several metal bars and small bells or clappers; shaken like a rattle in ceremonies to frighten away evil spirits and to draw the attention of the *Neteru*. It is always depicted as the tool of a priestess or queen. Some sistra have at the handle a face of Het-hert; others have kittens or cats atop the loop or inside it at the bottom in honor of Bast.

TWO LANDS/TWIN LANDS

Geographically, Lower and Upper Kemet; metaphorically, the interconnected "lands" of *Neteru* and human beings; a living symbol of the interdependent natures of the secular and the sacred (see Introduction, footnote 1).

UASET

"Dominion," the Kemetic name of the city of Thebes, national capital of the most illustrious period of Kemetic history, the New Kingdom.

WEB (U'EB)

"Pure," the title of a priest(ess) whose temple duty is to assure the ritual purity and cleanliness of sacred rooms, tools and persons.

Reprint compiled by Stargazer Design
2328 E. Lincoln Highway, Suite 108
New Lenox, IL 60451

Made in the USA
Lexington, KY
13 July 2018